THE
TRAINING NEEDS ANALYSIS
POCKETBOOK

By Paul Donovan and John Townsend

Drawings by Phil Hailstone

"Concise yet comprehensive, a handy and valua___ ___ing professionals."
Justin Kinnear, Education & Training Manage___

"Paul and John have done a fabulous job in illu___
analysis has to align the resultant training soluti___ ___f
the target organisation."
Bernard Foley, Training Officer, American Int___

"Accurate, precise, thorough and an invaluable tool for anyone involved ___
training and development needs."
Brian Kirwan, Human Resources Director, Irish Blood Transfusion Service

Published by:
Management Pocketbooks Ltd
Laurel House, Station Approach, Alresford, Hants SO24 9JH, U.K.
Tel: +44 (0)1962 735573   Fax: +44 (0)1962 733637
E-mail: sales@pocketbook.co.uk
Website: www.pocketbook.co.uk

This edition published 2004. Reprinted 2005, 2007, 2009.

© Paul Donovan and John Townsend 2004.

British Library Cataloguing-in-Publication Data – A catalogue record for this book is available from the British Library.

ISBN   978 1 903776 247

Design, typesetting and graphics by **efex ltd**. Printed in U.K.

CONTENTS

1NTRODUCTION

DEFINITION

Training needs analysis is identifying the new knowledge, skills and attitudes which people require to meet their own and their organisation's development needs.

PURPOSE AND FORMAT

The purpose of this pocketbook is to simplify training needs analysis.
You may have the impression that TNA (as we'll abbreviate it in the book), is a rather boring, time-consuming and somewhat bureaucratic process. We hope to show you that it can be strategic, rewarding, career-enhancing and even…fun!

To simplify things even more, we've divided the book into three main sections:

- **The training needs investigation** – an easy-to-follow process using the mnemonic INVESTIGATE which will take you through all the steps of a professional TNA

- **The ten point training plan** – the document, spreadsheet or wall chart where you can record all your notes from the training needs investigation and plan for each training course or event

- **The tool box** – crammed full of instruments, methods, tips and techniques to help you do a great job at every step of the TNA process

STORY

Once upon a time a competent young training manager of a fairly large manufacturing company was asked to do a professional analysis of the training needs of all the organisation's 5000 employees. What a great job she did!

Skills matrices were completed for all the operators and checked with each of them for accuracy, as well as in-depth interviews to analyse competency gaps for the office staff and the managers. Armed with an ocean of data, her department designed and organised the delivery of a series of top-class training courses – each one created with behaviourally stated learning objectives to help participants close their competency/skills, knowledge and attitude gaps.

The end-of-course evaluation sheets completed by every participant showed unanimous satisfaction with an average overall score of four out of five.

However, three months after the training courses had all been completed, the president of the firm called the training manager to his office and told her that company results were **worse** than they had been before the training!

INTRODUCTION

WHAT WENT WRONG?

Following an investigation into what went wrong the young training manager was able to establish:

- Insufficient connection between the training design and the mission of the organisation. The mission wasn't clearly defined so the training that was delivered missed the mark

- A lack of focus on the business goals and objectives that training could have supported

- The existing culture was resistant to the changes being put forward in the training, eg people were **rewarded** for rapid output while being **trained** to slow down and improve quality

- The organisation's structures and processes did not support the training messages (eg 14 layers of hierarchy existed while the training emphasised the empowerment of staff)

- The technology needed to implement the new skills was not available back on the job

- The company compensation system rewarded individual effort whereas the training concentrated on teamwork

INTRODUCTION

RESEARCH RESULTS

One investigation in the USA* suggested that 90% of all training is a waste of time and money for one of three reasons:

- Like the story on the earlier page, the training is not transferred to the job – either for cultural reasons (no interest or reward from the organisation for people to change their behaviour and apply the learning) – or structural reasons (barriers to or lack of opportunity to use new skills)

- Training design and/or delivery is poor and therefore not seen as useful or relevant

- The participants are not willing, able or 'needy' to learn

Detterman and Sternberg, 1993.

INTRODUCTION

STAKEHOLDERS – WHAT'S THEIR ROLE?

SENIOR MANAGEMENT	To tell us what their goals are so we know what to concentrate on.
LINE MANAGEMENT	To help us turn the organisation's goals into performance requirements and learning objectives, and to identify gaps in team and individual performance.
TRAINING DEPARTMENT	To develop a training and development policy for the organisation, to drive a training needs investigation and to turn learning objectives into learning opportunities.
JOB HOLDERS	To identify gaps in their own performance and to help in the search to close them.

NOTES

THE TRAINING NEEDS INVESTIGATION

THE TRAINING NEEDS INVESTIGATION

INVESTIGATE

I dentify key priorities

N ew performance goals

V isualise what will help and hinder

E liminate obstacles

S earch for alternative solutions other than training

T raining solutions

I ndicators of success

G aps in people's competence

A ssure relevance of content

T ransfer of learning

E valuation of training

THE TRAINING NEEDS INVESTIGATION

COMMON-SENSE STEPS

In order to simplify the TNA process and make it work in your organisation, we suggest you conduct a training needs investigation.

In other words, work through a series of common-sense steps, asking challenging questions to various people in the organisation as you proceed – a bit like any investigator or consultant trying to find out what's happened or what's needed.

The INVESTIGATE approach will help you avoid falling into the same trap as the training manager in the story on page 8.

IDENTIFY KEY PRIORITIES

As a starting point for your training needs investigation you'll need somehow to get access to the CEO/senior manager/key decision-maker in your organisation.
The reason for this is that any training that you ever design and deliver needs to link into whatever the organisation is trying to do. If it doesn't, you'll be like a ship without a compass or a house without foundations....and you may end up just being known as 'that nice person in Training'.

On the next page are a few challenging questions that we've found useful in teasing out organisational priorities from leaders and creating credibility for the training function.

IDENTIFY KEY PRIORITIES

POSSIBLE QUESTIONS FOR THE SENIOR MANAGER

- What, at **this** moment, is your key priority?
- What are your strategic/organisational/business goals for the next 12 months?
- What work issues keep you awake at night?
- How will you define today's success in a year's time?
- If you could whisper in the ear of every front-line person, what would you say?

17

IDENTIFY KEY PRIORITIES

INTERVIEW TAKE-AWAY

What will you take away from your interview with the senior manager?

You now know where to focus your energy and resources. Your notes will show you how to help line management prioritise their people's training needs and put their money into actions which will deliver results relating to their own objectives.

Your notes will also help prevent you using the 'hosepipe' approach to training, ie the random spraying of training all over the organisation.

THE TRAINING NEEDS INVESTIGATION

NEW PERFORMANCE GOALS

Following your information gathering session with the senior manager, you should now try to find out from line management **who** should do **what differently** in order to meet the strategic goals you have just uncovered. What are the new tasks? What new skills will be required to do these things well?

It's at this point that you take the organisation's priorities and elaborate them into measurable competencies.

For help with this process see the Tool Box section: pages 49-57 on competencies and pages 75-76 on focus groups.

New PERFORMANCE GOALS

CHALLENGING QUESTIONS FOR LINE MANAGEMENT

Here are some challenging questions for you to ask as you help line managers to articulate their ideas on new performance goals:

- Which of the areas of under-performance in your organisation have no obvious explanation in terms of market or environmental conditions?

- In what ways do people who work for our competition out-perform us?

- If you were a customer, which area of our customer service would you find most frustrating?

- Who is a role model in area XYZ and why?

- If you could be left with only one skill in this department, which one would it be?

- What's the most desirable trait you look for in a new hire?

- What, in our people, do our competitors most fear/respect?

VISUALISE WHAT WILL HELP AND HINDER

Now that you have established the new performance needs with line management, it's important to recognise that, however enthusiastic and positive they are about their people acquiring the new knowledge, skills and attitudes needed, there may be a number of obstacles in their way.

Whether or not you eventually identify training as being the best way to help reach the new performance goals, you need to analyse the forces at work which will help and hinder people changing and adopting new ways of doing things. Otherwise you might launch into costly actions which lead to no change in performance.

One of the most effective ways of visualising these forces is to use a force field analysis tool. This tried and trusted method is explained in the Tool Box section on page 45.

ELIMINATE THE OBSTACLES

Some of the obstacles you will identify during your force field analysis will have obvious solutions. For example: lack of resources; customer-unfriendly billing/delivery system/service; office layout; pay and bonus system, etc.

Others may be more complex, for example cultural resistance to change.

So here's where you plan how to clear the way and ensure that people will be able to learn and **use** new knowledge, skills, attitudes and/or values. Your job is to signal to line management that the obstacles, whatever their nature, will act as a brake on the performance of people and will, therefore, limit the effectiveness of training. In some cases training may even be counter-productive by raising expectations which cannot be met.

It may sound funny, but sometimes you may have to argue **against** training because you fear for its success. These are the moments when you become a real 'performance consultant'!

THE TRAINING NEEDS INVESTIGATION

SEARCH FOR ALTERNATIVE SOLUTIONS

You are now left with a set of feasible performance improvement targets. Before recommending training, you should first look for alternative and more efficient solutions to these needs.

SELL MORE	PRODUCE MORE	WASTE LESS
Instead of training:	Instead of training:	Instead of training:
• Introduce bonus scheme	• Introduce pay for production scheme	• Improve production process
• Simplify sales admin	• Reorganise production layout	• Use better materials
• Advertise	• Introduce flexitime	• Invest in technology
• Offer discounts	• Invest in new machinery	• Hire more qualified people

TRAINING SOLUTIONS

Having looked for alternative solutions, the next step is to identify the remaining performance issues for which training *is* the answer. In other words, when it becomes obvious from your investigation that improving people's knowledge, skills and attitudes is the key to meeting the new performance goals, then you recommend training.

At this stage you'll want to take a 'broad brush' approach and get the line managers to outline the kind of training they think will best help people develop the new competencies. You'll obviously have some ideas of your own.

When you've pinpointed the areas for training, things will start to get serious and you'll need to agree on some indicators for success; some specific learning objectives that you'll be able to measure **after** the training. And how will you know what to set as learning objectives? Read on!

INDICATORS OF SUCCESS – LEARNING OBJECTIVES

Now you need to concentrate on the things you can train people to do, to know and to value. Your objective is to leave the meeting with the line manager with objectives – **learning objectives**!

To learn how to write these you can go to the Tool Box section on pages 77-78.

Questions which will help elicit learning objectives from line managers might include:

- What specifically will people be able to do differently when the training is over?
- What competencies will they be able to display?
- What will you accept as evidence that the learning has been successful?

For tips on writing **competencies** please go to the Tool Box section on pages 49-53. Other methods for quantifying the learning needed include using **focus groups** and **stakeholder analysis**. Examples of these can be found in the Tool Box section on pages 68-69.

THE TRAINING NEEDS INVESTIGATION

GAPS IN PEOPLE'S COMPETENCE

This step in the transfer needs investigation is where most people start – ie finding out who needs/wants training in what. That's why a lot of training fails. If you don't take the seven previous steps in your investigation, training may end up as *nice to have* but not tied to the organisation's purpose and priorities and therefore irrelevant.

In your meetings with line management you've narrowed certain areas down to the essential. Given your research so far, you now need to know **which individuals need how much training** in these areas. The tools you can use here include:

- A competency audit
- A skills audit (also known as versatility charts)
- Interviews
- Observation
- Questionnaires

- Performance appraisals
- Requests for training from individuals
- 360° surveys
- Knowledge and skills tests
- Attitude surveys

You'll find examples of how to create and administer these tools in the Tool Box section on pages 55-66.

ASSURE RELEVANCE OF CONTENT

Something that many trainers forget to do is to ask the people who know what performance they want to help design the training that will provide it. Too often line managers are kept isolated from what is included in the content of the training courses because this is seen as the preserve of the trainer. As a result, you may get the wrong things being taught.

Here are some tips to help assure that training design is relevant and usable:

- Senior management to sponsor every programme
- Senior management to intervene at least once on every course (in person, in writing or on video)
- Line managers to sign-off on learning objectives and content outline
- Line managers to proofread trainer guides
- Managers to open and close programmes
- Some well-qualified managers to teach on certain modules
- Managers to attend courses during breaks/lunches to discuss how things are going

TRANSFER OF LEARNING

One of the big disappointments in training is the lack of transfer from the training room back into the workplace.

It could be too late to worry about this after the training is completed. So it is at this point in the investigation that you plan how to manage the transfer process. We call this process the 'learning transfer bridge' or the '8Ps'. And it's important that the bridge be under construction **before** the training begins.

For more about the 8Ps of learning transfer see the Tool Box section on pages 79-95.

EVALUATION OF TRAINING

Why should training evaluation appear in a book on training needs analysis?

Well, evaluation starts with the identification of training needs because, unless you are clear on what you want to achieve with training, you won't be able to measure whether you have succeeded. Suffice it to say that the design of your evaluation process should happen **now** (see also the Tool Box section on page 96).

Whatever you want to test/check when the training has been completed, the instrument you will use **then** needs to be put in place **now**.

- Do you want to test people's reactions to the training with a 'happy sheet'? What specifically will you try and measure with that sheet?
- Do you want to test their learning somehow? How about seeing if people actually put the training into practice and change their behaviour three to six months later?
- You'll probably want to know if the line manager's performance goals have been met…will you need a special measurement device for this or will you take his/her word for it? Or maybe performance improvement will be self-evident.

For details on how to evaluate the various levels of training impact see *The Training Evaluation Pocketbook* in this series.

NOTES

THE TEN POINT
TRAINING PLAN

THE TEN POINT TRAINING PLAN

DESCRIPTION

The **ten point training plan** is a document that will help you to record the results of your training needs investigation and how you intend to put into practice the learning objectives you identified.

The plan could take the form of a report, a spreadsheet or even a wall chart.

In total the ten elements of a good training plan are:

1 Vision/mission/strategy

2 Performance issue being addressed

3 Specific learning objectives

4 Participant categories

5 Methods of participant selection

6 Outline of training solution (course(s))

7 Who will deliver the training?

8 Training delivery standards

9 Roles and responsibilities

10 Evaluation criteria

THE TEN POINT TRAINING PLAN

WHAT TO INCLUDE

VISION/MISSION/STRATEGY

Assuming that your organisation has a published vision/mission/strategy statement you need first to find an extract from it which endorses, justifies and validates the need for the kind of training you are planning to develop, and then include it at the beginning of your ten point plan.

If your organisation does not have a written vision, mission and strategy then it's useful to try to elicit what they are – they do exist, you know! You can find out by asking a few questions and by seeking some documents that should be available within your organisation.

The organisation's **vision** can be identified by interviewing the CEO and by trying to find out how he/she *sees* the firm now and into the future. What is their *picture* of the firm? Ask them to describe it in vivid terms. If a vision has not been drawn up for your organisation, the answers that you get may well be vague and unspecific. Don't give up. Keep asking, *'Why this?'*, *'Why that?'* Ask your CEO to explain to you what purpose, apart from making money or providing such and such services, the organisation fulfils. The more you persist the more clear it will become.

WHAT TO INCLUDE

1 VISION/MISSION/STRATEGY (Cont'd)

Establishing an organisation's **mission and strategy** is really about asking five questions. These are:

1. What products and/or services does the organisation provide? What market or public sector is it in?

2. How does it provide those services? In what way does it position itself in this market? What beliefs and values drive the way it conducts its activities?

3. Who does it provide these benefits for? Who are the customers and consumers?

4. Who does it use to provide them? Who are its allies and strategic collaborators including its own suppliers?

5. Why does it supply these benefits? What is its overall purpose?

WHAT TO INCLUDE

PERFORMANCE ISSUE BEING ADDRESSED

One way of making sure that your training solution hits the mark is to remind yourself constantly of the performance issues the training is trying to deal with (see page 24). This is, if you will, the 'title' section for each planned course or intervention.

WHAT TO INCLUDE

SPECIFIC LEARNING OBJECTIVES

You will draw these course/intervention learning objectives from the results of your training needs investigation (see page 25).

It's critical to keep these objectives in the front of your mind as well as in the front of the training plan. Always remind yourself that many training initiatives (90%?) come to nought because of failure to carry the precise intent of the learning objectives agreed with line management into the training design.

WHAT TO INCLUDE

4 PARTICIPANT CATEGORIES

This section of your training plan covers the types/groups of employees who will be targeted for this training. It will also detail categories that may be excluded from the training.

You'll obviously get this information from your training needs investigation notes (see page 26).

WHAT TO INCLUDE

5 METHODS OF PARTICIPANT SELECTION

This will be a key and relatively lengthy section of your training plan. In order to choose actual participants from the employee categories targeted, you will need to decide on the 'gap identification tools', which will show you which people are lacking which knowledge, skills or attitudes in terms of the new performance goals.

The reader of your training plan will want to know how you decided on the contents of the training and how/why individual participants will be selected to attend.

In this section, therefore, you should describe the whole of the INVESTIGATE process as well as the gap identification tools you have chosen from pages 55-74 of the Tool Box section of this book (for example: competency audit, interviews, skills matrix, performance appraisal, etc).

WHAT TO INCLUDE

 6 OUTLINE OF TRAINING SOLUTION

This section of your plan will be more or less detailed depending on how many training events you are planning. The level of detail may vary from:

- Course title, sub-title and learning objectives

to

- A complete description of each module

WHAT TO INCLUDE

7 WHO WILL DELIVER THE TRAINING?

In this section you should include the names
and CVs of the trainers who will deliver your
courses. The CVs should contain enough
information to justify their selection and
be open to challenge by managers and
participants.

THE TEN POINT TRAINING PLAN

WHAT TO INCLUDE

TRAINING DELIVERY STANDARDS

This part should be a standard element of every training plan, and could even be pre-printed. It represents the organisation's required level of quality concerning:

- Course joining instructions
- Venue management
- Professional training delivery

(See also *The Trainer Standards Pocketbook* for ideas on how to set up your own internal training standards.)

WHAT TO INCLUDE

9 ROLES AND RESPONSIBILITIES

In this section of the training plan it's important to outline the roles and responsibilities of the main triangle of stakeholders involved in training, because training transfer is often spoilt by a failure of one of the parties to fulfil their role:

- **Participant** – prepare personal learning objectives for the course; be present 100% of time; participate enthusiastically; attend pre- and post-course briefings and follow-up meetings with boss and/or trainer

- **Training department** – conduct the training needs investigation; draw up training plans; administer joining instructions; organise and supervise delivery of training; conduct evaluations and follow-up

- **Manager** – participate in the training needs investigation; support and brief participants before, during and after the training; set measurable objectives and reward the practice of learning

WHAT TO INCLUDE

 EVALUATION CRITERIA

This last part of the training plan is where you describe the criteria and the process that you have agreed with line management will be used to evaluate the success of the training.

This will ensure that you are protected against 'moving goal posts', revisionism and bad faith following the training event.

It can also help to focus everyone's attention on transfer because when you are clear on what to evaluate it is so much easier to organise for success!

See the Tool Box section on pages 96-97 for a summary of the four levels of training evaluation, or *The Training Evaluation Pocketbook* in this series for more detail on how to measure training success.

NOTES

TOOL BOX

FORCE FIELD ANALYSIS
DEFINITION AND METHODOLOGY

Force field analysis (FFA) is a simple method for visualising the things that will help or hinder any proposed change, so that you can plan for **realistic** implementation of your actions. In the training needs investigation, FFA can be used at the **'V'** stage when you need to visualise what will help and hinder people as they learn, and try to apply, new knowledge, skills and attitudes.

How?
● Write the **new performance goal** on the top of a flipchart/pinboard

● Divide the sheet in two: **Help** and **Hinder**

● Brainstorm on Post-its all the things which are 'enablers' and will help people change, and those 'obstacles' which may stand in their way

(See examples on next two pages.)

FORCE FIELD ANALYSIS

EXAMPLE 1

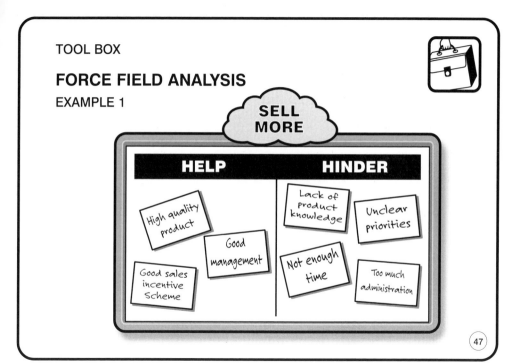

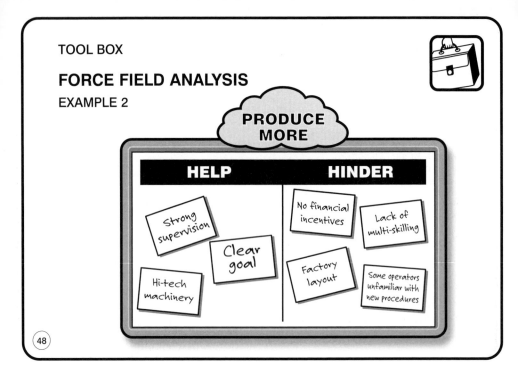

TOOL BOX

FORCE FIELD ANALYSIS
EXAMPLE 2

PRODUCE MORE

HELP	HINDER
Strong supervision	No financial incentives
Clear goal	Lack of multi-skilling
Hi-tech machinery	Factory layout
	Some operators unfamiliar with new procedures

TOOL BOX

COMPETENCIES

DEFINITION

In this section, we're going to show you how to describe, 'dose' (see page 52) and find ways to strengthen competencies before going on to look at how you can measure people's 'gaps'.

To keep it simple we've defined competencies as:

The behaviour patterns, based on acquired knowledge, skills and attitudes, which a person needs to bring to a job in order to carry out certain key tasks with competence.

So, when we define new performance goals we need to elaborate new competencies.

COMPETENCIES
HOW TO DESCRIBE THEM

Once key tasks have been identified for a job, a good competency description will meet the following criteria:

- Behaviourally stated (how people should do things)

- Observable and measurable

- Culturally congruent (should reflect the organisational culture)

- Stand-alone (no overlaps with other competencies)

TOOL BOX

COMPETENCIES
EXAMPLE FOR AIRPORT SECURITY EMPLOYEE

KEY TASK

Checks boarding passes, tickets and permits in order to detect fraud and ensure airline and airport security

COMPETENCY

- Questions passengers and staff courteously but assertively

- Recognises validity of all tickets, boarding passes and other airport permits for travel or access to terminals

MEASURE

- Averages 80% on the checklist of agreed courteous and assertive behaviours made by observer

- 90% accuracy of recognition during spot check by manager

TOOL BOX

COMPETENCIES
'DOSES' OF COMPETENCE

To 'dose' a competence simply means to describe
the various amounts of ability and skills needed
to deliver performance in a key task area.

In other words, **describe the kind of
knowledge, skills and attitudes
demonstrated by people who are:**

Developing this competence
Operational in this competence
Strong in this competence
Excellent in this competence

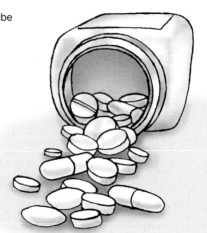

TOOL BOX

COMPETENCIES
'DOSES' OF COMPETENCE

EXAMPLE FOR AIRPORT SECURITY EMPLOYEE

COMPETENCY

Questions passengers and staff courteously but assertively	KEY TASK Checks boarding passes and permits

Developing	Checks documents in a perfunctory manner. Questions people impersonally without warmth or politeness.
Operational	Same as level one but with personal eye contact and politeness.
Strong	Checks documents, asks questions with a smile and addresses people as 'Sir' or 'Madam' (if possible 'Mr or Ms XYZ').
Excellent	Creates a warm 'moment of truth' – ie treats each individual as a special and valued customer. Enquires about their journey and engages in brief, friendly banter.

COMPETENCIES
HOW TO STRENGTHEN THEM

Training may be only one of literally hundreds of ways to help people strengthen their competencies.

We suggest the use of a focus group (see page 75) as one solution. Call together a group of people specialised in the competency in question and brainstorm creative/cost-effective activities which will accelerate the development of the necessary knowledge, skills and attitudes.

COMPETENCIES

COMPETENCY AUDIT

A competency audit is a way of identifying the gaps in an individual's competence at performing their key tasks.

As part of TNA, the competency audit will help you find out **who** needs **what** development in the areas which have been highlighted in your training needs investigation.

TOOL BOX

COMPETENCIES

COMPETENCY AUDIT: EXAMPLE 1 – Airport Security Employee

KEY TASK: Checks boarding passes and permits

COMPETENCY	IMPORTANCE TO JOB (1-5)	Developing ? Operational ? Strong ? Excellent ?
Questions passengers and staff courteously but assertively.		
Recognises validity of all tickets, boarding passes and other airport permits.		

TOOL BOX

COMPETENCIES

COMPETENCY AUDIT: EXAMPLE 2 – Team Manager

KEY TASK: Facilitates team meetings

COMPETENCY	IMPORTANCE TO JOB (1-5)	**D**eveloping ? **O**perational ? **S**trong ? **E**xcellent ?
Suggests meeting agenda and processes for problem-solving and decision-making.		
Listens actively by checking understanding and agreement of others.		

IDENTIFYING COMPETENCY GAPS
SKILLS MATRIX (aka VERSATILITY CHARTS)

Skills matrices are means of recording and consolidating the skill levels of any number of team members across a range of skill areas. A skills matrix can be completed using the boss's judgement only or by using a participatory approach with team members.

Legend: No Knowledge or Skills · Basic knowledge · Some experience · Competent under supervision · Fully competent

NAME	Induction completed	Safety training completed	Word Processing	Cash Accounting	Reception	Filing	Inter-personal	E-mail	Action
O'Connor	✓	✓							Word Processing/E-mail course next Autumn
Reilly	✓								Intensive training to catch up with team
Khan	✓	✓							E-mail course next Autumn
Sullivan	✓	✓							E-mail course next Autumn
Donovan	✓								E-mail course next Autumn
Lopez		✓							Word Processing/E-mail course next Autumn

IDENTIFYING COMPETENCY GAPS
STRUCTURED INTERVIEWS

There are hundreds of formats for establishing competency gaps at the individual level, using interviews, surveys and questionnaires.

Structured interviews, carried out by the training professional/performance consultant with individuals who have been targeted as needing to meet new performance goals, are time-consuming but rewarding. Rewarding because well-constructed questions can help you ensure that you end up with real training needs based on real, accepted gaps in people's skills and not just 'wants'.

Good interviews also help you avoid conducting 'wall-to-wall carpeting' or 'sheep dip' type training where everyone has to go to a course whether or not they need it. Part of the purported 90% of wasted training comes from teaching people things they already know or that they don't really need for their jobs.

(This kind of training can be justified, though, when the CEO sincerely wants all employees to attend an event as part of a company 'values identification' drive.)

IDENTIFYING COMPETENCY GAPS
STRUCTURED INTERVIEWS – EXAMPLE

Opening Question:
'Under the following headings, what training would help you become effective in meeting your new performance goals?'

Technical, job-related training?	
How specifically will this help you?	
Interpersonal skills training?	
How specifically will this help you?	
Information?	
What information do you need and how will it help you exactly?	

IDENTIFYING COMPETENCY GAPS
360° QUESTIONNAIRES

Getting feedback from 'all around' a person (ie from boss, colleagues and subordinates as well as from the individual) can give a much clearer and fairer picture of that individual's development needs than feedback from just a single source.

360° surveys on individuals are expensive and time-consuming and are usually reserved for senior management. However, the relatively low risk aspect of acting only on consensus points means that subsequent training action is tailor-made to the job and to the organisation's needs.

IDENTIFYING COMPETENCY GAPS

360° QUESTIONNAIRES – SAMPLE

How does the person you are scoring rate on the following issue?
Please mark an x on the line.
(1 = Low, 5 = High)

1	**2**	**3**	**4**	**5**

IDENTIFYING COMPETENCY GAPS

360° QUESTIONNAIRES – SAMPLE RESULT

Question 25. Providing a vision for the team

Respondent 1	Respondent 2	Respondent 3	Respondent 4	Respondent 5	Respondent 6	Your average for this question	Average for managers in this organisation	Your assessment of yourself
4	3	1	2	5	3	3	3.2	4

TOOL BOX

IDENTIFYING COMPETENCY GAPS

ATTITUDE SURVEYS

Attitude or climate surveys are excellent tools for establishing how well-equipped and motivated people are to deliver expected performance. This is because such surveys give feedback not only about how the employees perceive the organisation, but also about what they think and believe.

So, with a well-designed survey, you can measure how much **knowledge** people (and exactly <u>which</u> people) have about the organisation and its goals; what **skills** certain groups of people are perceived to have and whether employee **attitudes** and **values** are in line with those outlined in the mission statement.

And of course, these surveys can be conducted **before training** to pinpoint the needs, and **after training** to measure its impact.

IDENTIFYING COMPETENCY GAPS

ATTITUDE SURVEYS – SAMPLE 1

12. I have confidence in the management team of this organisation (please circle your answer).

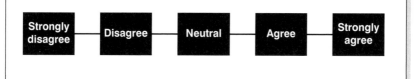

IDENTIFYING COMPETENCY GAPS

ATTITUDE SURVEYS – SAMPLE 2

32. Please describe what it's like to work in this organisation in terms of your own day-to-day experience.

....

....

....

....

....

....

....

IDENTIFYING COMPETENCY GAPS
OBSERVATION

Observation is the most 'hands-on' way to satisfy yourself regarding the training needs of your potential course participants. There are two main approaches to observation:

Overt
This is where the individual knows they are being observed as they carry out a certain task. This approach has the advantage of openness and honesty. However it can sometimes alter the true level of performance because of issues unrelated to training (eg fear of management, trying to impress, or simply being in the spotlight, like in the famous Hawthorne experiments).

Covert
This is where you observe someone but don't let them know they're being watched or listened to. This has the advantage of giving you a view of uninhibited performance, but is morally questionable in most cases. Exceptions could include jobs where public safety is involved or other critical jobs where incumbents agree to unannounced spot checks on their behaviour. For example, 'help-desk' employees who accept that any of their phone calls with customers could be recorded 'for quality purposes'.

IDENTIFYING COMPETENCY GAPS
STAKEHOLDER ANALYSIS

Stakeholders are individuals and groups who have an interest in the performance of the target group for your training.

- Everyone has a **customer** for the work they do, even if that customer is someone internal in the organisation

- Everybody has **people who depend upon them** for product, services or support

Often, these stakeholders can be a rich and speedy source of information to back up and verify some of your assumptions about training needs. The question you will specifically be asking the stakeholders is:

'What do you think these people need in terms of knowledge, skills and attitudes that will help them to meet the new performance goals?'

IDENTIFYING COMPETENCY GAPS
STAKEHOLDER ANALYSIS – WHO TO ASK?

- These stakeholders can be contacted personally or by email to save time
- Some of their views will be more important than others so you will need to weight and prioritise your inputs

IDENTIFYING COMPETENCY GAPS

KNOWLEDGE PRE-TESTS

The best way to find out if someone knows something is to ask them! Tests can be conducted at the beginning of a course to establish the gap in participants' knowledge of what you're going to teach them or, better still, before they actually come on the course so that you only train those who need the training. Example of a knowledge pre-test:

MOTIVATION THEORY TEST

1. Maslow described:　　Four ❑　　　　Two ❑　　　　Six ❑

   levels of motivation *(please check one)*

2. Adam's Equity Theory deals with expectancy　　　TRUE　　　FALSE

   (Please circle one)

TOOL BOX

IDENTIFYING COMPETENCY GAPS
PERFORMANCE APPRAISAL – DEFINITION

A regular (usually annual) review of a person's performance against targets and standards, carried out by their boss, who first completes an appraisal form (see page 74) and then holds a structured two-way interview with the person. In many organisations these days the annual appraisal interview includes an 'upward' appraisal where the employees also rates and gives feedback to the boss.

A well-designed and well-conducted appraisal system is the simplest and most cost-effective way of identifying competency gaps, as long as there is clarity about:

- The job to be done
- The progress that is being made
- The competencies required to meet new performance goals
- The 'dose' of competence required to fill the gaps between present and desired performance in the new goal areas
- The type of knowledge, skills and/or attitude training that could help fill those gaps

TOOL BOX

IDENTIFYING COMPETENCY GAPS
PERFORMANCE APPRAISAL – COMPONENTS

To conduct a performance appraisal effectively you need:

- **A job profile** form to give clarity about the role of the person being appraised (see next page)

- **Interim appraisal notes** – notes made on performance issues and incidents discussed at quarterly appraisal meetings to ensure fair and unbiased coverage of annual performance when the time comes

- **Annual appraisal form** – a template for conducting the annual appraisal session with each team member (see page 74)

IDENTIFYING COMPETENCY GAPS
PERFORMANCE APPRAISAL – JOB PROFILE

A typical job profile form looks something like this:

Name of job ....

Purpose of job ....

Short-term goals ....

Long-term goals ....

Key result areas ....

Key tasks ....

Competencies needed to perform tasks satisfactorily

....

IDENTIFYING COMPETENCY GAPS

PERFORMANCE APPRAISAL – ANNUAL APPRAISAL FORM

A typical appraisal form contains:

- Admin details
- Job objectives and results achieved
- Standards of performance for on-going tasks and performance achieved
- Descriptions of competencies needed to perform tasks satisfactorily and rating on each one
- Space for job holder's comments on ratings
- Training and development needs and plans to meet them
- Actions agreed

TOOL BOX

FOCUS GROUPS

Focus groups are just what they sound like – groups of people who come together to focus on an issue with a view to resolving a problem or deciding something. They usually get together in short-burst meetings of up to 90 minutes which are facilitated using an agreed format.

As far as TNA is concerned, focus groups could be used for:

- Identifying competencies that a group of employees need to develop in order to meet new performance goals

- Brainstorming the many ways particular competencies can be developed/ strengthened

TOOL BOX

FOCUS GROUPS
FACILITATING FOCUS GROUPS

1. Start with a 'focus' question to inspire interest and/or identify how much people know/don't know about the topic. You can represent this on a flipchart and ask members to step forward and place a mark at the level that corresponds to their position on the issue.

2. Ask a 'discussion' question such as, *'What are the competencies we need to develop in communication?'* or, *'How can we develop the competency, "**communicates well with customers**"?'*

3. Ask members to write ideas on separate cards so that you can cluster them on a board.

4. Create actionable items from card clusters.

WRITING LEARNING OBJECTIVES

The best way to write learning objectives is to think of the acronym **SAS**.

SITUATION What situation will the learner be in when they are demonstrating that they can do this task skillfully?

ACTION What specifically will they be able to do when the training session is over?

STANDARD Some measure by which we will be able to judge success

TOOL BOX

WRITING LEARNING OBJECTIVES

EXAMPLE

By the end of this training session:

SITUATION Given a calculator
and the day's
takings.....

ACTION participants will be
able to balance the
cash book.....

STANDARD to 100% accuracy

THE LEARNING TRANSFER BRIDGE (8Ps)

There's no point in doing TNA unless what gets trained gets transferred – transferred back to the workplace in the form of improved performance. Although you, as the training professional, can't be held fully responsible for designing and managing the transfer process, you can influence its success. Here are eight things that need to be in place as a 'bridge' back to the participant's job to help make training work. We call them the 8Ps:

1. **Performance Improvement Plan** for each individual in the organisation.
2. **Participation of line management** in the design and delivery of training.
3. **Pre-course briefings** between participants and their bosses.
4. **Preparation of learning logs** to chart individuals' progress in learning.
5. **Programme support** before, during and after the training.
6. **Post-course briefing** between participants and their bosses.
7. **Peer and team support** after training.
8. **Prizes and sanctions** to reward new behaviour and sanction lack of it.

TOOL BOX

THE LEARNING TRANSFER BRIDGE (8Ps)

 1. PERFORMANCE IMPROVEMENT PLAN

Human performance improvement starts with a plan. As trainers we are responsible, along with line management, for making sure that every individual has an opportunity at least once a year to talk to their manager about how to do things better – *how to* means being given new performance targets. The results of this discussion, whether it takes place as part of the annual appraisal or at a separate meeting, should be recorded on the Performance Improvement Plan (PIP). Keep the PIP simple but include the following:

- **LINK** How does this person's performance link with and contribute to the overall performance of the organisation?

- **GAP** What is the gap between the person's present performance and the standards, objectives, new performance goals for the job. How was the gap measured? (See Identifying Competency Gaps on pages 58-74)

TOOL BOX

THE LEARNING TRANSFER BRIDGE (8Ps)

1. PERFORMANCE IMPROVEMENT PLAN (Cont'd)

- **SOLUTIONS** What training does the person need to help bring about improved performance? What other development activities should be planned (job rotation, secondment, promotion, etc)? What other non-training actions might help (salary increase, job enrichment, process changes, etc)?

- **RESOURCES NEEDED** What are the costs of these actions in terms of money, equipment, staffing, etc?

- **OBSTACLES** Be realistic! What things will be hindering the achievement of the plan (environment, culture, motivation of others, etc)?

- **MEASUREMENT** Finally, how will improvement be measured and rewarded (objectives, follow-up, etc)?

TOOL BOX

THE LEARNING TRANSFER BRIDGE (8Ps)

 2. PARTICIPATION OF LINE MANAGEMENT

As we saw under 'Assure relevance of content' (the 'A' of INVESTIGATE), line managers' inputs are vital when we start to create training solutions for filling performance gaps. Here are some guidelines:

- Get managers to sign-off on the learning objectives which you will use to design the learning events

- Note down how the learning process in the courses you are designing will deliver what managers expect

THE LEARNING TRANSFER BRIDGE (8Ps)

2. PARTICIPATION OF LINE MANAGEMENT (Cont'd)

- Train managers to contribute at least one module to each course. OK, so they're not very professional trainers, but you can limit a potential 'delivery disaster' by providing your exercises, or by 'topping and tailing' the sessions with your own input. Even if managers are not as good as you are at giving punchy training messages, the results will at least be linked to what they really want and need – and therefore they will know what behaviours they will measure and reward back on the job.

- If this is not realistic in terms of managers' skills and/or availability, ask them (cajole, coax, blackmail!) at least to open and close training events. This will lend credibility and impact to the training, as will impromptu, interested visits by managers to training courses. Apart from anything else, this involvement keeps managers in tune with what training is trying to do to help **them** help their people to improve.

THE LEARNING TRANSFER BRIDGE (8Ps)

3. PRE-COURSE BRIEFINGS

This is one of the most valuable steps in making sure that learning is transferred into performance improvement. Honestly speaking, how many participants on your training courses have had serious, job-related briefing sessions with their bosses before they come? How many have discussed their mutual expectations as to what they will learn and how they will put it into practice back on the job?

Your role as a trainer is to make sure these briefings take place. It's the old story, isn't it? Unless someone knows what is expected of them how will they know whether they've achieved anything?

TOOL BOX

THE LEARNING TRANSFER BRIDGE (8Ps)

3. PRE-COURSE BRIEFINGS (Cont'd)

One of the best ways to conduct a pre-course briefing is to use the PIP (Performance Improvement Plan) or to refer back to the most recent appraisal discussion and to define some key learning objectives for the course. You can help managers to set clear, behaviourally stated targets and insist that they agree on a date for a post-course briefing (see page 90).

Here are some examples of typical objectives formulated at a pre-course briefing.

At the end of this course the trainee will:

- Be able to use the new XYZ software
- Have learned and practised new presentation techniques
- Have acquired the knowledge about new EU regulations in order to modify ABC
- Be able to explain the new mission and values statement to the team
- Know and have practised the steps involved in a good selection interview

Maybe you should insist upon signed evidence that a pre-course briefing has taken place before you allow anyone to attend a course! Sometimes, by making something more difficult to have, you make it more desirable.

THE LEARNING TRANSFER BRIDGE (8Ps)

4. PREPARATION OF LEARNING LOGS

In order to allow people to track their progress as they acquire new knowledge, skills and attitudes, many organisations have introduced individual **learning logs**. These logs provide people with an on-going record of their learning achievements and of the steps they are taking/still need to take on the journey to improved performance.

There's an example of what could be covered in such a document on the next page.

TOOL BOX

COURSE LEARNING LOG

1. **Expectations** – what am I expected to achieve/do before, during and after the course?

2. **Manager's role** – how will s/he provide support?

3. **Trainer's role** – how can the trainer help me most?

4. **My learning objectives** – based on the course learning objectives. How to measure?

5. **Notes from pre-course briefing** – details of discussion with my boss.

6. **Course notes** – notes on learning, spot evaluations of relevance, satisfaction, etc.

7. **Learning achievements** – what did I actually learn? How can I prove it?

8. **Action plans from post-course briefing** – performance objectives set during post-course briefing.

9. **Obstacles** – things/people/environmental issues, etc that could be working against achieving these objectives.

10. **Plans to overcome these obstacles** – how can my boss/colleagues help me?

THE LEARNING TRANSFER BRIDGE (8Ps)

5. PROGRAMME SUPPORT

There is no doubt that current training lowers current productivity. People can't attend a course **and** do their jobs at 100% efficiency. Nor should they be expected to get back to 100% immediately after a course. They should have some time to practise the new learning.

This is not easy because it often means a change of attitude from both the manager and the trainee. In some cases it also means a change in the culture of the organisation from 'training as a perk' to 'training as a vital investment for growth'.

THE LEARNING TRANSFER BRIDGE (8Ps)

5. PROGRAMME SUPPORT (Cont'd)

Before a course As a trainer, you should be coaching managers on how to create an environment where people like learning. Managers could start by setting a good example – by being learning individuals themselves. Just as with learning organisations, managers need to encourage learning every day, in meetings, discussions, appraisals. They can do this by asking questions, reviewing PIPs regularly, commenting on their own learning, etc. On the practical side, both the manager and the trainee should be planning **how to cover the trainee's job** during the learning to avoid stress and worry.

During a course Above all, the boss should **leave the trainee in peace** during the training! No phone calls for information. No frantic emails. On the contrary, maybe a note or call of encouragement during the course, or, even better, a lightning visit to the training venue for a chat on how it's going.

After a course Because most people these days are overloaded with work, they often have to put off practising new skills and techniques until that magic day when they will suddenly have enough time. Managers and trainers need to recognise that the implementation of learning will require that some tasks be reallocated, or quite simply postponed, so that the trainee can concentrate on trying out the new skills.

THE LEARNING TRANSFER BRIDGE (8Ps)

6. POST-COURSE BRIEFINGS

All the research data on the transfer of learning says, *'The longer you wait, the less you will use it'*. So, the first few days following any learning event are a vital time.
As soon as possible after the course, the trainee and their boss should sit down and talk about how to put the new knowledge, skills and/or attitudes into practice – basing their discussion on the pre-course briefing (see pages 84-85).

Specifically this will mean:

- Turning pre-course learning objectives into performance objectives

- Identifying obstacles to achieving these objectives and starting to plan how to overcome them. Don't forget that many of these plans may involve peer and team support (see pages 92-93)

.....and noting everything on the trainee's learning log!

THE LEARNING TRANSFER BRIDGE (8Ps)

6. POST-COURSE BRIEFINGS (Cont'd)

Examples of learning objectives (see page 85) turned into performance objectives following a course:

1. All my sales reports will be produced on XYZ software by the year end.
2. My next three presentations will have been structured using the newly learned model, and the feedback sheet I distribute will show a score of over three out of five for 'body language'.
3. By July 31st we'll have rewritten our ABC procedures in line with new EU legislation.
4. I will have conducted two 'mission and values' meetings with my team before the end of September and obtained an 80% commitment to the statement.
5. By October 31st, an observer will have confirmed that at least two selection interviews I conducted followed the steps learned.

Examples of obstacles to achieving objectives two and four:

- Time/opportunity to practise (objective two)
- Acceptability of feedback sheet to audience (objective two)
- Acceptability to team members of 'being told values' (objective four)

THE LEARNING TRANSFER BRIDGE (8Ps)

7. PEER AND TEAM SUPPORT

As we saw in the post-course briefing session (previous page), trainees' bosses will have worked with them to set objectives for putting training into practice in the workplace and will have helped to identify obstacles to doing this.

In order to help overcome these obstacles (noted on the trainee's learning log) the boss will have to take a team approach. One approach is to organise **sharing sessions** when a team member returns from a training course. The trainee presents the key learning points to his/her colleagues and discusses the relevance of this learning to the job. The learning log can then be used to jot down **agreements on the support which each colleague will provide**.

THE LEARNING TRANSFER BRIDGE (8Ps)

7. PEER AND TEAM SUPPORT (Cont'd)

Because the trainee will need time and space to practise, the manager should help to restructure his/her workload. As mentioned on page 89 under Programme Support, this may mean temporarily allocating certain of the trainee's tasks to other team members (whether or not they volunteer!).

The manager might also provide support by establishing learning pairs within the team. A learning pair is simply two team members who have attended the same training event, and whose job is to compare notes on the effectiveness of the training received and to support each other as they try to put the learning to work.

TOOL BOX

THE LEARNING TRANSFER BRIDGE (8Ps)

8. PRIZES AND SANCTIONS

It's sad but true that, most of the time, in most organisations, most people are not specifically rewarded for putting into practice what they learned in training. On the contrary, they're sometimes actually *punished* for trying to!

- *'Enjoyed the holiday? Now back to the real world'*

- *'Don't rock the boat now, just because you've been on a fancy training programme'*

- *'We're not having any of that 'touchy-feely' stuff in this department, I can tell you!'*

- *'We'd love to use these new systems but we simply can't afford the equipment needed'*

TOOL BOX

THE LEARNING TRANSFER BRIDGE (8Ps)

8. PRIZES AND SANCTIONS (Cont'd)

Just imagine how much more seriously training would be taken if people's salaries (or even just their bonuses) were dependent on them putting into practice what they learned on courses!

Without going that far, prizes for new behaviours come in many forms:

- Salary increases
- Bonus payments
- Praise and recognition
- New and more interesting projects
- Higher quality of working life

And, as a last thought, how could you 'sanction' people for not doing what they learned in training? That's where your motivational creativity comes in!

TOOL BOX

EVALUATION

THE FOUR LEVELS

In 1959, Donald Kirkpatrick published a series of articles on training evaluation in the journal of the American Society for Training and Development (now known as ASTD). The four levels of evaluation were born.

Since then they have stood the test of time and, although they have been 'tweaked' and added to over the years, they remain the basic tool for trainers to assess whether their training is effective. The four levels are summarised on the next page. For more details on training evaluation please refer to *The Training Evaluation Pocketbook*.

TOOL BOX

EVALUATION

THE FOUR LEVELS

- **REACTION** Did the participants like the course? The famous 'happy sheet'. Get all participants to complete one at the end of each course

- **LEARNING** Did the participants learn anything? Test their knowledge, skills and/or attitudes toward the topic at the end of the training. If you want to be sure that the training caused the learning you have to test them at the beginning too!

- **BEHAVIOUR** Did the participants change their behaviour as a result of the training? Test the behaviour after the training: probably three to six months later to allow the changes to kick in

- **RESULTS** Were the organisation's results affected positively by the training, as per the CEO's expectations from your training needs investigation?

NOTES

QUESTIONNAIRE

How easy will it be to make TNA
work for you?

EXPLANATION OF QUESTIONNAIRE

This questionnaire comprises 30 questions for you to ask of your organisation. The questions concern human resource systems and techniques which help to smooth the way for a good training needs analysis.

For each question you simply answer 'Yes', 'No' or 'Not Applicable'.

On page 108 you'll find out how to score and what your scores mean in terms of how easy it's going to be to make TNA work for you.

STANDARDS OF PERFORMANCE

		Yes	No	N/A
1.	Are organisational performance standards clear (eg production targets, quality requirements, etc)?			
2.	Are objectives set for all staff and related to organisational targets?			
3.	Are performance standards set for each job?			
4.	Have core competencies been defined for the organisation?			
5.	Have core competencies been defined for specific jobs?			
6.	Are long-term training needs identified at a strategic level, linked to long-term goals?			

MEASUREMENT SYSTEM

	Yes	No	N/A
7. Is the organisation's performance measured (eg production targets, quality requirements, etc)?			
8. Do shortfalls in organisational performance get analysed for training requirements?			
9. Is each individual's performance in meeting their objectives measured?			
10. Are people monitored for their achievement of on-going performance standards?			
11. Are people measured against the core competencies for their role?			
12. Are people's shortfalls in performance analysed for training needs?			

MANAGER'S ROLE

	Yes	No	N/A
13. Do managers regularly communicate business plans, strategies, goals to their team?			
14. Are managers held accountable for the development of their staff?			
15. Is informal coaching part of the culture of the organisation?			
16. Is an appraisal system in place in the organisation?			
17. Do people get regular and accurate feedback from managers about their performance?			
18. Does the appraisal system generate personal development plans for everyone?			

REWARD SYSTEM

		Yes	No	N/A
19.	Is good performance rewarded?			
20.	Is the reward system fair and consistent?			
21.	Does the reward system include options like extra responsibility, career development opportunities, training, etc.?			

Well Done!

CAREER PLANNING AND DEVELOPMENT

	Yes	No	N/A
22. Are individual's career aspirations understood and planned for?			
23. Do people get feedback on career development issues?			
24. Are training needs for career development identified and addressed?			

SUCCESSION PLANNING

	Yes	No	N/A
25. Are future job demands for the organisation understood?			
26. Is there an up-to-date succession plan for the organisation/ departments?			
27. Are managers held responsible for training and developing their people for succession purposes?			

QUESTIONNAIRE

RECRUITMENT AND SELECTION

	Yes	No	N/A
28. Is there a consistent and robust recruitment and selection process in place?			
29. Are candidates' skill/competency levels matched to job demands when recruiting?			
30. Is there a well-designed and useful induction programme?			

QUESTIONNAIRE

SCORING

How easy will it be for you to make TNA work in your organisation? Well, the better the human resource systems in place, the easier it will be for you to establish training needs and provide **sustainable** solutions.

Please count the number of 'Yes' answers you've given on the questionnaire.

25-30 Great chances of a smooth ride!

15-25 You may have to work on improving some HR systems before hoping for total success.

10-15 Lack of underpinning from HR systems could make it tough to get enough good data from your training needs investigation.

0-10 An uphill struggle could be looming – unless you are also the HR Manager and are in a start-up phase!

About the Author

Paul Donovan MSc (Mgmt.)
Paul is Head of Programmes with the Irish Management Institute in Dublin where he is responsible for a suite of training and development programmes for HRD professionals. He has extensive management experience and has conducted a wide range of HRD assignments in Western Europe and Asia.

Paul's professional interests include researching evaluation of training and development interventions where he has identified easy-to-use surrogate measures as effective replacements for time-consuming and expensive evaluation initiatives. He has edited seven books in a series of management texts.

Contact
Paul Donovan can be contacted at: Irish Management Institute, Sandyford, Dublin 16, Ireland.
Tel: 353 1 2078474   E-mail: donovanp@imi.ie

About the Author

John Townsend, BA MA MCIPD

John has built a reputation internationally as a leading trainer of trainers. He is the founder of the highly-regarded Master Trainer Institute, a total learning facility located just outside Geneva which draws trainers and facilitators from around the world. He set up the Institute after 30 years' experience in international consulting and human resource management positions in the UK, France, the United States and Switzerland.

From 1978–1984 he was European Director of Executive Development with GTE in Geneva with training responsibility for over 800 managers in some 15 countries. John has published a number of management and professional guides and regularly contributes articles to leading management and training journals.

Contact:

The Master Trainer Institute, L'Avant Centre, 13 chemin du Levant, Ferney-Voltaire, France
Tel: (33) 450 42 84 16   Fax: (33) 450 40 57 37   www.mt-institute.com

THE MANAGEMENT POCKETBOOK SERIES

Pocketbooks (also available in e-book format)

360 Degree Feedback
Absence Management
Appraisals
Assertiveness
Balance Sheet
Business Planning
Business Writing
Call Centre Customer Care
Career Transition
Coaching
Communicator's
Competencies
Creative Manager's
C.R.M.
Cross-cultural Business
Customer Service
Decision-making
Delegation
Developing People
Diversity
Emotional Intelligence
Employment Law
Empowerment
Energy and Well-being
Facilitator's

Flexible Workplace
Handling Complaints
Icebreakers
Impact & Presence
Improving Efficiency
Improving Profitability
Induction
Influencing
International Trade
Interviewer's
I.T. Trainer's
Key Account Manager's
Leadership
Learner's
Management Models
Manager's
Managing Budgets
Managing Cashflow
Managing Change
Managing Customer Service
Managing Difficult Participants
Managing Recruitment
Managing Upwards
Managing Your Appraisal
Marketing

Meetings
Mentoring
Motivation
Negotiator's
Networking
NLP
Nurturing Innovation
Openers & Closers
People Manager's
Performance Management
Personal Success
Positive Mental Attitude
Presentations
Problem Behaviour
Problem Solving
Project Management
Psychometric Testing
Resolving Conflict
Reward
Sales Excellence
Salesperson's
Self-managed Development
Starting In Management
Strategy
Stress

Succeeding at Interviews
Talent Management
Teambuilding Activities
Teamworking
Telephone Skills
Telesales
Thinker's
Time Management
Trainer Standards
Trainer's
Training Evaluation
Training Needs Analysis
Virtual Teams
Vocal Skills
Working Relationships
Workplace Politics

Pocketfiles

Trainer's Blue Pocketfile of
Ready-to-use Activities

Trainer's Green Pocketfile of
Ready-to-use Activities

Trainer's Red Pocketfile of
Ready-to-use Activities

22.05.09

ORDER FORM

Your details

Name _____

Position _____

Company _____

Address _____

_____

_____

Telephone _____

Fax _____

E-mail _____

VAT No. (EC companies) _____

Your Order Ref _____

Please send me:

		No. copies
The Training Needs Analysis Pocketbook		
The _____ Pocketbook		
The _____ Pocketbook		
The _____ Pocketbook		

Order by Post
MANAGEMENT POCKETBOOKS LTD
LAUREL HOUSE, STATION APPROACH,
ALRESFORD, HAMPSHIRE SO24 9JH UK

Order by Phone, Fax or Internet
Telephone: +44 (0)1962 735573
Facsimile: +44 (0)1962 733637
E-mail: sales@pocketbook.co.uk
Web: www.pocketbook.co.uk

Customers in USA should contact:
Management Pocketbooks
2427 Bond Street, University Park, IL 60466
Telephone: 866 620 6944 Facsimile: 708 534 7803
E-mail: mp.orders@ware-pak.com
Web: www.managementpocketbooks.com

CARDIFF AND VALE COLLEGE